Christmas Joy

Jenpu H. Back

Christmas Joy

Let
Heaven and Nature
Sing

George H. Back

Spirit & Intelligence Press, LLC

Text Copright © 2007 by George H. Back

All rights reserved. Published by:
Spirit & Intelligence Press
Oklahoma City, OK

ChristmasJoyBook.com

Library of Congress Catalog Number: Pending

ISBN: 978-0-9800520-0-8

FIRST EDITION

Printed in the United States of America

Acknowledgements

In 2002 the Wardens and Vestry gave to me the publication of "Back Talk" as a gift during a celebration of my twenty years as Dean of St. Paul's Cathedral. This book is based in these writings. I abide thankful for this gift and for the many other ways the people of St. Paul's have blessed my life.

I am especially thankful to Frank Dennis, Steve Parker and Melba Rhinehart for originally starting this publication process and to David Wright, Mike and Brooke Murphy who have recently moved it along. I have enjoyed working with Grey Allman as editor, with Clanci Miller-Arrow on page design and proofing, with Kell Miller-Arrow on graphic optimization and with Bruce Pearce on printing. Appreciation also goes to David Coffey, Anne Kueteman and Meredith Back for artwork. Gary Derrick and Susan Urbach have been most helpful in the publishing process. Clergy colleagues and Cathedral staff have been generously patient with my oft-distracted presence.

Acknowledgements for this book must go back to our Creator and creation. My parents, godparents, grandparents, extended family and friends, long before conscious memory, provided an environment friendly to a child's spiritual affections. The gift of Heather, Luke and Geordie, as children and adults, has added blessings beyond any description. In addition there abide grandchildren and parish children, tiny treasures that continue to brighten both daily life and special occasions.

I would have escaped much of my soul-education with babies and small children had I been left to my own academic disposition. I am thankful to Margaret for forty years of life together and for the 'baby friendly' zeal that she has manifested in many forms. These include her professional medical work as an international Lactation Consultant; her reaching out to sick infants, anxious parents, at-risk and abused children; her hosting of fun parties, children's teas, food fights, and numerous other child friendly gatherings. She has been a child advocate of immense energy and irresistible enthusiasm.

I am thankful to our gracious Creator for all that is above and beyond words.

Table of Contents

Preface	1
Battle for Truth	3
Will Christmas Ever Come?	5
Surprise Me	7
Barn Phew & Church Pew	9
Womb Prayer	12
Aiden & His Newborn Grandfather	16
Don't Jiggle	19
Baby Jesus as Spiritual Guide	21
Touching Baby Flesh	24
Toddler Faith	27
Absolution & Peace	30
Yes, Virginia, Jesus Loves Santa Claus	32
A Christmas Absent	34
A Dickens of a Christmas	37
Imagination	41
Scuffy	44
Sock It To Me	46
Suppose	49
Tight Receivers	51
Faith Is Fun	53
Child Power	56
Primal Lover	59

Christmas Music	62
Potato Party	65
Clarity	68
Have a Great Body	71
One Light	74
Recovering Light	77
Terror & The Innocents	81
Noisy Night	85
At Home	88
"Fa-la-la-ing"	91
Joy to the World	94

Beware of
The Draggin' of
Toomuchstuff

Preface

I was slowly picking my way through the stacks of old books in what seemed like a deserted area of the seminary library. I was soon to complete my master's degree in theology, and I was missing something I desperately wanted to know. I was searching for "soul."

Words such as "mind" and "ego" corresponded to something I thought I knew. But "soul" was a word that seemed somewhere "out there" in space or "back there" in time. Was soul real? I was too ashamed to ask the question aloud. My searches ended in frustration. The essence of soul stayed hidden among a vast assortment of questionable ideas.

Christians, Jews, Muslims, Buddhists, Hindus, other believers, and non-believers are of similar body and brain at birth. Differences of ideas and beliefs emerge as we mature. By spending time with babies and small children, by contemplating life from the perspective of this beginning point, we can discover the depth of soul. We may also appreciate an original unity of soul shared at this depth by all humanity.

Soul is not realized through rational thought, but through our "trust-faith" that precedes knowledge and beliefs. It is the natural abode of the spirit — our primal center — and it transcends the limitations of mere words and ideas. When a baby receives positive, nurturing care, trust-faith manifests itself in love and joy. The same is true of soul.

It seems ironic, if not comical, that I should write a book about how soul cannot be found through the ideas communicated in books. Like a baby who wakes up at the most inconvenient of times, reality disrupts our attempts to equate truth with rationality. Soul can never be explained, proved, or defined by the mind.

Christmas Joy: Let Heaven and Nature Sing is about renewing our lives by harkening back to our primal condition, as infants and children. It is about appreciating the "worth-ship" of a baby as revealed and adored in the Christ Child. As we enter into communion with our childlike qualities, issues of worldly and religious contention fade. The distinction between the "self" and the "soul" our Lord created becomes smaller.

Play along for a while, and you may hear a baby's voice crying out, "Regress, return, and rejoice in trust-faith. The Light shining in darkness will light up your soul. Let heaven and nature sing together in your heart!"

Battle for Truth

At Christmastime we set up a crèche in front of our house. When our granddaughter Louisa was two years old, we attempted to tell her that its figures were Mary, Joseph, and baby Jesus. She would have none of that revisionist history. She sternly rebuked us, pointing at the figures and proclaiming, "Mommy! Daddy! Baby!" All additional attempts to identify the crèche figures led to theological warfare.

Louisa, like Martin Luther, "Here I stand!"

We could have invited science to intervene and settle the argument with facts, but science would only conclude these things to be sculpted poly-resin acetate forms. Scientific information, while it is concise and precise, would be most useless in this instance.

Whatever names we were contending over, all such controversy was created out of our own frames of reference. Louisa did not mistake these figures for a real mommy, daddy, and baby anymore than we mistook them for the real Mary, Joseph, and Jesus. The battle was not about the tangibly real figures, but about their meaning and significance. Louisa's view of the truth was not to be shaken by our strange adjustments to the obvious.

As a child in New York, I loved to visit the Hayden Planetarium. When I learned the planet Jupiter was named after a Roman god, I presumed that the ancient Romans were not too bright. I imagined them worshiping this strangely colored ball in the sky. I later discovered that *piter* in "Jupiter" referred to *pater*, Latin for "father." I was perplexed. Did the Romans really mean father as in "Our Father" or as in "Yur-pater"?

Our intelligence gives us the freedom to ponder truth, whether it's a particular truth, generic truth, or tangible truth. Those who do not ponder such things will likely think that truth may be grasped like a personal possession.

Mary, Joseph, and baby Jesus; Louisa's mommy, daddy, and baby; contemporary Americans and ancient Romans — they all share a divine origin even if we have grown up into differing beliefs. Our common humanity and our shared primal immaturity are Christmas presents a baby can give to us.

Will Christmas Ever Come?

Do you remember "child time" — the slow movement of time, hour after hour, day after day, waiting for the arrival of a special time? St. Paul teaches, "Do not ignore this one fact, beloved, that with the Lord one day is like a thousand years, and a thousand years are like one day" (2 Pet. 3:8).

Unlike the long Christmas wait of childhood, I have the contemporary adult experience of rushing time. Christmas comes at me like a speeding train — *woo-woo, chig, chig, chig, chig, chig* — except I'm still working on the tracks. The cards are not mailed; the gifts are not wrapped; the decorations are not up. *Chig, chig, chig, chig, chig, woo-woo.*

Woe, woe, woe says the book of Revelation.

Woe, woe to the earth and the sea, for the devil has come down to you with great wrath, because he knows that his time is short. (Rev. 12:12)

You are on Satan's shopping list of souls. He wants to give you a "devil of a time," scattering you in all directions. He is annoyed. Only thirteen more shopping days 'til Christmas. He wonders, "Can I still make this the worst Christmas ever?"

Shortness of time promotes intensity, obsession, and compulsion. It escalates the need for immediate gratification. The fast-thinking brain provides no salvation from such acceleration into fragmentation. Like the gas peddle to road rage, the exploitation of time is the expressway to frustration. There is no time for grief, sorrow, pain, or heartbreak. Hell is the quickest way anywhere.

"Real slow" seems like forever to a child, and it may be as close as adults can get to understanding the terms "eternal" and "everlasting." When we walk into church, we learn to move "real slow." When we approach the altar, we pause and then perhaps bow or kneel. When we are being holy, gentle, or intimate, or when we are listening to something strange and mysterious, we are practicing to be "real slow."

"Be still and know that I am God," says the Lord. You cannot hear this message if you are moving faster than the speed of sound. "Real slow" is the motion that brings us to the edge of this world and to the fringe of heaven. As we enter into the presence of God, there is no better place to be and no place better to move toward, so we stop. This is the present moment, the eternal now. It is "Christmas present" whenever human flesh and God are here at the same time.

Surprise Me

One year my older sister asked for a bicycle. I don't remember what I asked for, but my parents knew that once Patti had a bike that I would soon want one also. That Christmas two bikes arrived, one for Patti and a bright blue one for me. It was a pure surprise.

The bike soon became the center of my world. In conspiring with other boys, it was obvious that the extra weight of various bicycle parts hampered the speed we desired. I made improvement upon improvement by removing part after part. I made the bike my own unique contraption. When I removed the chain guard, my father warned, "You'll catch your pant cuff in the chain." "No I won't!" I said. Again and again I would be surprised when my pant cuff was caught in the bike chain.

It was not cool to have fenders on your bike because they weighed it down and slowed it up. I still remember the refreshing day when I discovered their purpose. The dirty wet stain down the center of my clothing proclaimed my baptism into the secret truth of traditional common sense. Of course, I still did not put the fenders back on.

From these experiences I was learning the adult art of standing firm in the error of my conviction. Resisting truth requires tenacious discipline and a willingness to suffer for a greater ignorance. I am obviously one who bears witness to the old quip, "You are never too old to do something stupid."

Spiritual maturity is realizing that what I have worked so hard to achieve is much less than what I deeply desire. My soul yearns to be known better and loved more than I know or love myself!

Today, my child-soul still hopes for a real surprise, like the one I received as a young boy. It wants to be known and loved by an Intelligence and a Lover that is higher, greater, purer, and truer than my self. I yearn to receive what I do not know enough to ask for.

Parents occasionally exceed a small child's Christmas expectations. However, it is not likely for any mortal human, or even for Santa Claus himself, to do this even occasionally for teens or adults.

While many of us struggle to give someone we love the perfect present, I find that thinking about it never gets me very far. I must depend on some gracious happenstance or some special inspiration. Giving is like dancing. When my head dominates my feelings, like when my brain commands my feet, gracefulness does not manifest itself.

Like a parent who knows that a boy would love a bicycle, God knows that our child-soul would love the presence of God's child. It is the gift beyond our expectations, one that surpasses thoughtful, rational, understanding, that is the ultimate Christmas surprise.

Barn Phew and Church Pew

Velvet ran up to me, all affection and no inhibition. Her filthy paws grabbed my arm as I tried to pet her. Being some mix of bloodhound and bird dog, she was not easily discouraged. She had no sensitivity to my finicky avoidance of saliva, mud, foliage, and fleas. Anyone who is familiar with the fussiness of small children or the ravages caused by lack of sanitation and hygiene will suspect that our contemporary sensitivities to the icky, sticky, and gross are necessarily natural.

I became aware of this when Margaret and I moved as newlyweds into an old New England house. It was built by a ship's carpenter around 1737. There was some speculation that it was constructed as a split-level house so the animals could live below and the humans above. The old basement, with its dirt floor and deep cistern, had somehow avoided the modifications of modernization. With only one thickness of pine board to separate the living quarters from the animal shelter, life for our colonial forebears would have been quite gamey. However, the shared warmth of beast and human during the long, cold winters might have been worth the close encounters of such crude a kind.

Tales of the 1700's indicate that many people (not only brides), carried bouquets of flowers. They were not for mere decorative beauty, but as a place of refuge for the nose. One could lift up the flowers and receive a reprieve from the overwhelming offensive odor of human crowds. The *bath*room was an obviously late addition to our old New England house.

What is the difference between a church pew and barn stall? Humans tend to exaggerate the difference between the two spaces, but angels might not make the "de-stink-tions" we make between ourselves and animals. We must all seem like similar carbon-based organic creatures to the heavenly extraterrestrials.

When St. Francis created for the world the Christmas manger scene to educate local peasants, he exemplified the place where the heavenly touches the earthy. In Christ's birth, we see the natural and the supernatural are united and distinct from the rational and ideological.

"You behave like you lived in a barn!" is rarely a compliment. Yet necessity makes for strange bedfellows, none stranger than the King of Heaven being born among farm animals. God was not so picky, finicky, or proud as to avoid all the fumes and foulness of human existence.

Would you tell the one born in a stable stall that a church pew is too uncomfortable? Would you say that you are too morally distinctive to associate with hypocrites? Christmas is about divine humility, a truth come down for our salvation.

Womb Prayer

From the time my daughter Heather was a small child, she loved church in a way anyone could see easily. During long church services she was generously patient with and tolerant of our boring adult habits. We would talk, talk, talk, but she knew that we should sing, pray, and march around. Still, she quietly suffered through our tedious, wordy, unnatural behavior. She was willing to wait in faith for adults to develop and learn how to enjoy playing Church together.

When we were expecting Luke, we bought a child's book about pregnancy and birth to read to two-year-old Heather. At one point, Heather's eyes lit up, as she pointed at a picture of a baby in the womb. "Look, it's praying!" she said.

Children notice things that adults often miss entirely. Our soul, our state of communion with God, comes forth from this aboriginal depth of our being. While adults jump to conclusions, children leap to beginnings.

St. Luke tells the story of Elizabeth, pregnant with John the Baptist, visiting Mary, pregnant with the Christ child.

When Elizabeth heard Mary's greeting, the child leaped in her womb. And Elizabeth was filled with the Holy Spirit. (Luke 1:41)

The Creator of our exquisitely sensitive humanity endows us with souls that rise to the greatest heights when called forth from the depths of another loving soul.

In many cultures, elders are the primary people of prayer. They are the ones who sit quietly at the gates of the next world and who connect the busy world of adults to the heavenly purposes of God. In fact, the word "priest" comes from the Greek word "presbyter," which means "elder." If we enter life praying, and we die praying, why don't we live our lives praying? Why do we live spiritually isolated from God and one another?

A baby needs nine months to develop. No baby would think itself clever to be born after only four months in the womb. We also must allow time to grow, to come to full-term, and to wait in faith for spiritual competence, so we can face the rigors of the world. Jesus frequently taught that his time had not yet come. Why should we think that our time is always here?

Babies can teach us much about prayer and about peace. They sleep even in the midst of noise and commotion. Baron Von Hugal taught about the Prayer of the Arab in the Sandstorm. When overwhelmed by a desert storm, a shepherd may curl up into the fetal position and wait for the storm to pass. When our feelings and senses are overwhelmed by the world, we, too, may curl up like a nut in a shell or a baby in the womb.

Christmas might be called "The Feast of the

Regression to God." Winter provides long, cold nights, perfect times for staying under warm covers. A little hibernation provides time and space for the primal spirit to brood over the chaotic waters of our own minds and bodies. Allowing this, we may rise into a bright morning, like we have been born anew.

Christmas is a time when remembrance is particularly powerful. Many people can remember at least one painful Christmas; some have Christmas memories only of chemical abuse, domestic violence, or heightened family conflicts. Many need a long prayerful period of "re-creation" to overcome such traumatic moments of being.

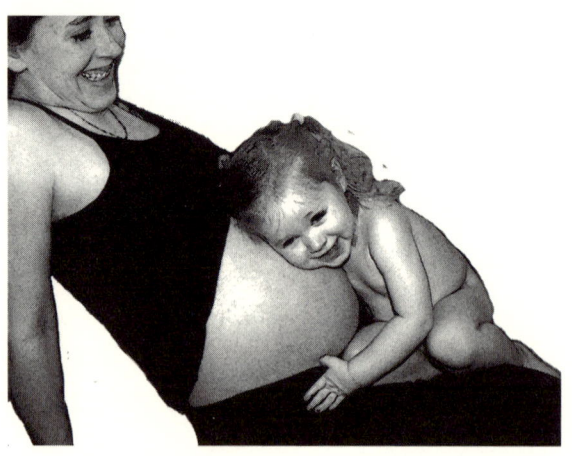

Louisa listening for Sims and Josh.

As we approach maturity, we must realize that our Creator provides us with two possible habits from which to choose. One habit is to worry. The other is to pray. Give voice to your soul. Pray. Allow the Creator to reform you from within. Choose the habit that lets your body become God's habitation.

Those willing to share a two-year-old's vision of reality can see faithful souls praying from deep within the womb of this wintry world. Christmas reveals that in our lowest earthly condition, even eking out survival among animals and their fodder, our existence is no abandoned effect from a careless cause. Rather, it is a fresh, bright, warm light that bursts through the darkness, like a seed into sunshine. Wherever that Light lightens, a soul leaps for joy.

Aidan and His Newborn Grandfather

As a new grandfather I fell deeply into the mystery of "baby love." This phenomenon is easily observed at social gatherings in which proud parents show off their newborns. At seven weeks old, our grandson, Aidan, came back from such a gathering with his little head covered in numerous shades of lipstick. He was obviously popular with the ladies.

Great-grandmother Grace and great-grandchild Aidan share a smile and an attitude.

What makes babies so lovable? They are not conversationalists, being good for only a gurgle or two. They don't tell stories, impart knowledge, or pay compliments. But the slightest smile from a baby sends ogling adults into delight.

Aidan has never achieved anything. He has never worked a day in his life. On the contrary he loudly demands "room service," day and night, with nothing too small or embarrassing for him to ask for. If he were an adult we would complain, "He behaves just like a baby!"

Like other infants, Aidan has skin that is so transparent that it is as if you can see through it to his human "beingness." Looking at him is like looking at a pristine soul before it is covered with the presumptions, exaggerations, distortions, and illusions that we have labored to learn ourselves and to teach to our children. What we see inside infants is something beautiful—we witness pure human nature. We catch a glimpse of our own hidden soul deep within, even though we may have smothered it beneath years of pollution. In babies we see open, almost naked soul. It is like a germinating seed filled with energy, freedom, and possibility. Here is the made-by-God human essence.

Aidan exhibits purity of faith. He does not doubt his self-worth. He does not condition his expression with the words "if it pleases you." He asks and expects to receive, seeks and expects to find. He assumes that he is loved completely and wholly. Woe, says Jesus, to you who teach God's children otherwise; your fate is to swim your life away with a millstone, a "death preserver," around your neck.

Aidan is filled with genetic information, millions of years old, passed on through the eons. He is prepared to engage a future filled with sights, sounds, words, images, stories, faces, and experiences of amazing diversity and complexity. Babies are magnificent creations, so very old and so freshly new.

Woe to those who impose their narrow knowledge or oppressive fears onto children. Blessed are they who let babies teach them the boundless love of God hidden in the flesh of humanity.

Don't Jiggle

Rejoice! Louisa Grace Back has arrived—7lb 8oz, born on October 14, 2004. Her mother, Meredith, and father, Luke, are happily adjusting to this powerful new being taking over their household.

To watch this complex, delicate and tenacious infant is to see naked soul revealed. Billions of years of divine information have gone into the production of this 2004 model. Like all of us, she is made in the image of God, exceeding all human art and surpassing all intellectual invention.

Her arrival in midst of community moves me to prophetic fire and zeal. Do not try to pacify a baby. The baby is at peace; you are the one who is uptight. Hold a baby in order to participate in its peace.

Please read this baby holding lesson: Never jiggle a baby with your arms. Imagine an 800-pound gorilla trying to get salt out of a saltshaker. That is what the baby feels when some huge adult jiggles it. Hold a baby gently and securely against one's heart. Then you may bounce, sway, rock, whatever moves you. Move your whole body, and let the baby move with you like a dance partner. Never move a baby faster than you would move your own torso.

The same is true about praying for people. Don't try to make something happen with some kind of mind force. Hold the person close to your soul, and ask God's blessing, healing, helping, whatever moves you. Love this person as yourself, and you can be a small portion of God's great love for that person.

Baby Jesus as Spiritual Guide

The Gospel of Luke tells the story about how Mary and Joseph brought baby Jesus into the temple when he was eight days old. Many old people like Simeon and Anna came to the temple in order spend their final days in the presence of God, then to die and be buried in that holy place.

When Jesus was brought as a baby into the temple, old Simeon and old Anna immediately saw what their souls yearned for. They had come to the holy place to complete their lives, and in looking at this newborn, they saw fulfillment of life. "Now let your servant depart in peace," proclaimed Simeon. What he meant was, "I have seen God's presence in this baby and now I am ready to be born from above." Birth and death, breathing in and breathing out, beginning and end, new and old — all these counterparts belong to one spiritual stream of divine grace.

The treasure of a pilgrim's soul lies in the immensity of its immaturity. Within this immaturity lies the possibility for freedom, growth and development.

Babies rejoice in spiritual incompleteness; they don't worry about their weakness and incompetence. A baby enjoys being merely a baby. Likewise, we should let our souls rejoice that we have so far to grow.

When Mary realizes that she is pregnant with God she sings the first Christmas carol. It is the song of one who is mired deep in a poverty of spirit, but who then recognizes the immense possibility of God alive within her. Like Anna and Simeon who came to die but see abundance of life, Mary sees the glory of God springing forth from the depths of her humility. So it is that Mary sings the words we now call "The *Magnificat*":

> *My soul magnifies the Lord,*
> *my spirit rejoices in God my Savior,*
> *for he regards the lowliness of his*
> *handmaiden.* (Luke 1:46-47)

The spiritual pilgrim will see in the baby a helpful guide. Babies live by grace, not by competence. They ask for food from the center of their hunger. Jesus teaches his followers to pray to his Father in heaven, who knows how to give good gifts to us. In Gospel parables he urges us to pester God—like the persistent widow who nags the dishonest judge, or like the host who annoys his neighbor in order to provide hospitality for a guest. Do not attempt to speak to God from a posture of confidence in your worthiness, but from your spiritual, intellectual and emotional neediness. Like Anna and Simeon, seek God in your dying. Like Mary, the unmarried-yet-expectant mother, seek God from your humiliation. Like a baby, cry deeply from an empty stomach, to be filled with the presence of God.

Touching Baby Flesh

At a local nursing home lives a resident who habitually cradles a doll in her arms. Why does this old woman, who is without mobility, without words, and without awareness of her environment, treasure this doll? Perhaps it brings back memories of holding a doll when she was a young girl. Perhaps she associates the doll with deep and tenacious feelings of affection and warmth. Perhaps the doll cues her to what her conscious mind has forgotten and elicits tender feelings that refresh her heart. Perhaps the doll is a source of peace, connecting her to a time when she could "sleep like a baby."

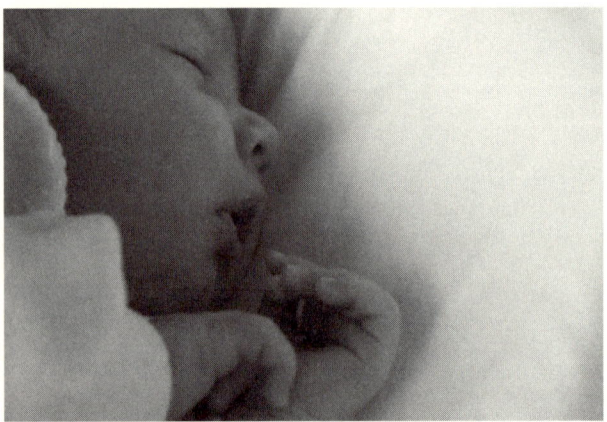

The contextual clues that the woman once used to inform herself about the world now fail her. In her disoriented adult life, she experiences reality like an infant. Babies cannot know why one minute they are cuddled and in another washed and stuck with a needle. For babies, people and events come and go as if by magic. Sounds pleasant or awful and sensations sharp or gentle each arrive and depart without warning. Just as a doll can comfort a small child, so it can also serve as a tiny anchor in a vast sea of what must often seem like an unknowable chaos.

One day I noticed a staff person tenderly holding the doll. Was the caregiver reaching out to the resident in one of the few ways that she could understand? Or was the staff member using the doll's likeness of a real baby to imitate her own affections for one? We seem naturally drawn toward such baby forms and child faces. Christmas images, such as that of the Madonna and child, encourage us to embrace the primal baby icon and what it represents to the soul.

I have seen old eyes light up from the sensation of holding a real baby. The feel of baby flesh is exceptionally soft, unconditioned by worldly anxiety. A baby provides us with physical and tactile awareness of what full relaxation can be. A baby is filled with peace, knowing no tension or conflict. Sometimes, when you look into the clear eyes of an infant, you can see your reflection, as if looking into a clean, pure lake at dawn. Flesh and soul meet in full harmony in the baby body.

Enfolding a sleeping baby in our arms tells us more about our humanity than a whole library ever could.

The baby's body has been given rubber-like flexibility, delicate strength, and tender toughness. There is no discipline that the adult body can practice, no adeptness at yoga or tai chi that an adult can master, that can produce such a magnificently balanced organism. Although we cannot recreate this perfection in our aging bodies, all spiritual and physical exercises that help us to imitate it are well worth the effort. By holding and touching babies, we become aware of what our own flesh should be like. Instead of seeking sculptured or rigid forms, we should embrace the exquisite sensitivity and flexibility of the baby's body as our ideal.

What does it mean to cherish a tender, lovable, "infantly-simple" soul? What is it to receive the presence of God at Christmas? The spiritual aspirant learns from the infant that it is through the dark density of this worldly womb that God informs us of what we shall become. To hold an infant's body is to touch a place on earth where the soul and the flesh are as one. If you ponder the likeness of your soul to a baby, you will learn about the terrifying vulnerability and awesome potential that abides within you. Where spirit touches flesh God's glory is revealed.

Toddler Faith

The first party of which I have the vaguest memory was not a Christmas party, but a block party. People brought out tables and chairs, food and drink to celebrate the end of the Second World War in the middle of the street.

I was only a toddler at the time. Although much of my future was being determined during the war, I had no cares or fears. Today, however, I am really competent at worrying about terrorism, cybercrime, destructive multinational institutions, global warming, financial disaster, food pollutions, and diseases of all sorts. My knowledge of these things has expanded more than my ability to do something about them. Should I not feel increased anxiety and frustration?

Many people watch the news religiously and repeatedly, while they pray sporadically and casually. They live their lives frozen in fear, rather than fluid in faith. Caution and foreboding lead the adult mind away from the energy, joy, and adventure that make the tottering life so much fun.

As a toddler wobbles between sharp table corners and electric appliances, she does not look behind her and doubt whether anything worthwhile is ahead.

But one thing I do, forgetting what lies behind and straining forward to what lies ahead, I press on ... let those of us who are mature be thus minded. (Phil. 3:13-15)

Although the toddler does not comprehend reality, which proves impossible to discover without pain, she presses on like a spiritual pilgrim. This is faith—the repeated presumption that I can make it across the room, maybe without smashing my head.

The flexibility of a toddler's body is appropriate for the physical rigors of learning to exist in a hard world. Similarly, the flexibility of human thought allows us to negotiate the difficulties of maturity. A rigid body would interfere with the toddler's development, just as a rigid mind inhibits the adult spiritual pilgrim. We are not here to create an ideal of perfection, but to move through a turbulent world toward the peace of God.

Come home from a day of trying to be the perfect business executive, realtor, clergy person, or whatever you do and deal with the toddler. Harder than that, stay home and attempt to be the perfect mother, father, or grandparent. No illusion of human distinction, dignity, or status stands before the dynamic onslaught of toddler chaos. There is no illusion in the toddler household that anything is under control.

Most adults are oppressed by idealism, trying to make Christmas be what they think it should be. It is like their brain is the locomotive and the rest of life make up the cars that trail behind. Unfortunately, many toddlers have been unable to cure their parents of this "train" of thought.

When toddlers are scared, they toddle right over to a parent for reassurance. When a stranger appears, they bury their heads in their mother's skirt or against their father's neck. Toddlers have great faith in these security sources.

Adults have a similar source of security in their religious faith when they pray "Abba," "Father," burying their souls into the depths of holy presence. The smart sneer that such a practice cannot provide real world protection from our world's overwhelming violence. At Christmas we see God's child enter into vulnerable space-time that is outside of anyone's control. It is in the reality of risk that the truth of faith must be born.

The infant Christ was born into a more dangerous world than many of us worry about today. Those who attempt to practice religion from strength and security will never understand the risks and vulnerability revealed on Christmas night.

Absolution & Peace

The wandering of Mary, Joseph, and Jesus through Egypt is similar to the experience that many contemporary people face living far away from family traditions and hometown roots. In our mobile society, we have traveled many physical and emotional miles from our childhood beginnings. Raising young children is heavy labor around the clock, and being far from home makes this experience more intense. Many people have no extended family nearby for support and assistance.

The sticky, dirty, drippy world of the toddler is a challenge to the sanity and energy of any adult. Attempts to keep a small child's clothes unstained and playspace ordered are usually frustrating and thankless tasks. Parents often feel angry or guilty when a small child's stubborn willfulness brings out a childish reaction in themselves.

It is here that parents must forgive their own selfish feelings, even as they forgive the tiny tyke twisting the ends of their shredded patience. There is one forgiveness for all of God's children, regardless of age and stage of life. We all need absolution from the sins of tyranny, our attempts to be gods in control of our own small worlds.

Is raising a toddler more enjoyment than work? Is our whole life more joy than labor? If we play god by trying to keep reality under control, then we allow heavy labor to become "job number one." If we can play with life and with the people around us, as small children play, then we can live with joy in our Creator's household.

Our lifelong spiritual challenge is evident when an exhausted and exhausting child will not close her eyes and allow us some peace. How easy it is to drive ourselves out of Eden, to allow the gift of a child become the responsibility of work. It is here that we must meet the toddler face to face, as child to child, as equal to equal, as soul to soul. Am I primarily a pain to my Creator? Am I really a joy?

Toddlers face an unknown world of immense uncertainties, but they also take delight in the world they explore. They cry immediately and fully at pain and failure; they accept joyfully almost everything else. If we can give up our own illusions of being adequate to handle the sins of the world, we can also love being alive. Our default attitude must not be grief over what might have been, or fear of what might happen, but toddler-like enthusiasm for whatever is happening now.

Many people live out their life spans as if they were life sentences. Having done their time, they are as thankful to God as most convicts are to their wardens. By being stuck in the past, or by fearing the future, they lose the childhood freedom to make fun out of the here and now. The same toddler who can try us down to the depth of our souls can also connect us to abundant life and the peace that surpasses all understanding.

Yes, Virginia, Jesus Loves Santa Claus

Oh you better watch out,
You better not cry,
You better not pout,
I'm telling you why.
Santa Claus is coming to town.

Don't let the bouncy tune fool you. The words are loaded.

He's making a list
And checking it twice,
He's gonna find out,
Whose naughty and nice.

The bookkeeping is precise. Not only does he have your number, but he is also omniscient.

He sees you when you're sleeping,
He knows when you're awake.

There is nothing you are going to get away with now.

He knows if you've been bad or good,
So be good for goodness' sake.

If you want to have a Merry Christmas, shape up!

How could such a cheerful little tune have such negative lyrics? One might just as well ask Scrooge to sing his great rendition of "I'm Dreaming of an Overachiever's Holiday."

We, too, can join in a top-secret propaganda strategy to keep children's high holiday spirits under control. Shhh, let's keep this quiet. Suppose children grow up thinking that they can receive something for nothing? They might end up living by grace instead of by labor. They might start celebrating what they receive, as if reality was some sort of great gift from on High. They might even start thinking that their lives were given for the holy and gracious expression of divine love!

Yes, Virginia, Jesus loves Santa Claus. Jesus loves Christmas parties; he always shows up with a bunch of extra guests. Jesus loves pouty, naughty children. Jesus even loves cranky adults who get too tired doing too much, trying to "make their own Christmas." Santa slyly adds some fun to the mental in order to make a truly "fun-to-mental" Christmas. Ho, Ho.

A Christmas Absent

Have you ever received a Christmas absent? If a present is an outward and visible sign of someone's inward and invisible love, then an "absent" is a material item given in place of real love and care.

How can you tell the difference between a Christmas absent and a Christmas present? Examining the material gift itself cannot reveal the truth. That would be like analyzing the ingredients in Communion bread to determine whether it is holy.

A gift from someone present does not preclude it from

being a Christmas absent. Some who are physically near to us may be distant in heart or spirit. A gift from someone who is far away might be an attempt to come spiritually closer, or it might be only a formal gesture.

A gift can be something that we send to replace ourselves, in the way a parent gives a toy to a child to keep the child from making demands on the parent's time. While it may be materially expensive, it is spiritually cheap to give an absent in place of a present. It is all too common for us to give a symbol of our affection while we keep time and attention for ourselves.

A Christmas present that honors the presence of divinity in the midst of humanity must bear the reality of our personal presence: our reaching out, our caring, and our willingness to spend ourselves for those we love.

No matter what the motivation is of the giver, no true gift can be received without the appropriate attitude of the receiver. The art of receiving a present requires accepting a gift in faith, hope, and love. To casually or thoughtlessly take ownership of an item reduces its meaning to a common transaction; it becomes merely a trade payment, or symbol.

We are capable of improving both our gift receiving and gift giving. We can extend our presence or bridge our absence through the medium of a gift. Learning to give and receive gifts with fidelity is no less spiritually challenging than praying and worshipping in spirit and truth.

Growing a consumer economy depends upon increasing the quantity of stuff transferred from one individual to another. Interpersonal communion depends upon using earthly gifts to share our faith, hope, and love. Struggling with our attitudes and feelings about Christmas gifts helps us to understand what is involved in fully receiving the many gifts from God.

For the first Christmas, humanity did not receive some *thing* dropped by airmail from heaven by an abstract and absent deity. We received a baby into our midst. We received God's presence, naked of all ideas, beliefs, and heavenly conditions. We received pure, personal, divine presence in the vulnerable and dependent form of baby flesh. The closest we may come to emulating God's Christmas presence to us is to give our fullest personal presence to God and to each other.

A Dickens of a Christmas

I know Christmas season has come when Margaret makes me sit down to watch a video of Charles Dickens's *A Christmas Carol*. My first reaction is "Humbug! I have seen this thirty-five times!" I would suspect some of you are reading these words because someone said, "Oh you hafta read this!" Although tempted, you knew better than to say "Humbug" aloud.

Margaret's favorite version of Dickens's *A Christmas Carol* is a black-and-white videotape with a crackling soundtrack; it is one of the earliest versions produced. Most of its actors were trained before the advent of talking films. Their gestures and expressions make much of the dialogue unnecessary. This is handy because you can barely hear the words.

The opening scene offers a panorama of London early in the 1800's. The camera shows a handcrafted model of St. Paul's Cathedral dominating the entire city, surrounded by small homes and businesses.

Dickens's story begins with a description of the primary character, Scrooge:

> Oh! But he was a tight-fisted hand at the grindstone, Scrooge! A squeezing, wrenching, grasping, scraping, clutching, covetous old sinner! Hard and sharp as

flint, from which no steel had ever struck out generous fire; secret, self-contained, and solitary as an oyster.

The cold within him froze his old features, nipped his pointed nose, shriveled his cheek, stiffened his gait; made his eyes red, his thin lips blue; and he spoke out shrewdly in his grating voice. …. He carried his own low temperature always about with him; he iced his office in the dog-days; and didn't thaw it one degree at Christmas.

Dickens's father had gone through bankruptcy, and Dickens spent much of his childhood laboring in workhouses for bleak survival. His writings became one of the most powerful forces in bringing some equity to the economic conditions that afflicted so many during his lifetime.

London has changed since Dickens was a child. Looking at the skyline of modern London, you would be hard-pressed to notice St. Paul's Cathedral. Numerous commercial buildings dwarf that shrine.

The same is true regarding economics and religion. In our modern age, economics dwarfs the religious. Economics is viewed as real, religion as made up. Let's think about this. Market forces, like spiritual forces, are not tangible entities. They exist as part of a complex, interactive network, intertwined with numerous other complex, interactive networks. They do not have a concrete existence like apples or molecules. No scientific instrument can detect a market force, yet the market dynamics are real, and economic forces exist everywhere.

Religion, like economics, is pervasive among humans. It is always there. Anyone who thinks that he or she can opt out of religion is similar to the one who willfully opts out of the economy.

When you pay some amount of money, or refuse to pay it, you are participating in setting economic values. By action or inaction, you always express the "worth-ship" not only of goods and services, but also of people and God. All behavior indicates an assessment of the worthiness of all that surrounds you.

Many people who think they are avoiding religion are actually practicing the religious equivalent of putting their money under the mattress. They will tell you, "You can't trust those organized, institutional banks (or religions) with all their rules and procedures. All they want is your money." Self-service economics and spirituality are equally wise.

Market forces continually give high prices to a vast quantity of trivial things. Choirs continually give glory to God. The author of *The Christmas Carol* continually gives "the dickens" to the wealthy.

Religion sees spiritual forces as angels; economics sees market forces as actual. What do people see when they see you? Are you Santa or Scrooge?

Why is it that Margaret keeps giving me another chance to watch Scrooge? Why did someone recommend this book to you? What gives, that I am continually asked to give? Why is it that all my choices are like stock, bought or sold in the divine economy? It is as if everything I do, and even don't do, counts!

Imagination

Did you know that I have won many athletic trophies in both golf and baseball? For me a three hundred yard drive and a hole-in-one were common occurrences. With the bases loaded, I hit many home runs and made the big difference in important games.

Of course, all of these events took place in my

Grandchild Joseph

youthful imagination. Actually, I could never keep my eye on the ball. I was always looking for where the ball should go and thinking of what would come next. Neither the golf ball nor the baseball ever paid any attention to my intentions.

I see people practicing religion in the same way. In their imaginations they do very well, but in reality they continually take their eyes off God. They sink like Peter — like a stone — into the depths of disappointment and negativity.

Spiritual attention to God must always be entwined with physical action. You must bring your material body to a material church building, if you are physically able. You must say your prayers with your material throat by making a physical noise. You might ultimately transcend such material necessity, but few people do.

Many people project their religion outside of reality without transcending anything. They become mental Tiger Woods of faith, while actually denying, rejecting, and avoiding the Creator of reality.

How do you know if you are worshipping a figment of your imagination or God? You don't need to know; you need to do! Truth is not choosing a better idea, but living in authentic love.

Imagined religion involves little time, little energy, little money, or little of anything tangible. It is isolated, sterile, heady, efficient, convenient, inexpensive, and sanitary. It appears superior to the public and visibly hypocritical practices of those who struggle with material religion. It abides untouched by reality and remains pure by the magic of invisibility to the worldly eye.

The Christmas message of "God in flesh" affirms the genesis and material creation of our humanity. The blunt, awkward reality is that we have been given a material body to be physically responsive to both our Creator and to one another. When we grow up and out of it, we have been promised a new but not yet visible spiritual body. But for our pilgrimage in this world, "what you see is what you got!"

Don't imagine that you are any more religious than what your body actualizes. Even after making a public, outward commitment of my body to God, I find fortresses in my mind stubbornly holding out against divine love and hindering actualization in this world. Faith does not give up on hope and love, because God is not only closer than my breath, but also deeper than my illusions.

Scuffy

As a child I loved the Little Golden Book called *Scuffy the Tugboat*. In this story, a small boy places a toy boat in a tiny brook. The boat then floats downstream and into increasingly larger and more dangerous waters. Carried by a river, the little boat comes into a large harbor where it precariously sails among huge ships. At the end of the story, the little boy retrieves the tugboat before it is lost into the ocean.

Can you see small Scuffy in an immense world?

As life has gained years, so this story has gained different meanings. Scientifically, if a drop of water falls from the sky upon a mountain, it might hit a rock and run down to join a few other drops and make a trickle. Numerous trickles might merge into a rivulet, and then into a brook, stream, and then a river.

The story might be about the human journey, life flowing from childhood into ever larger and swifter rivers of youth. When we enter adulthood the current may bring us to a great port at the river's mouth, filled with human motion, pollution, business, and traffic. Beyond the harbor and past land's end lies the great deep, the dark unknown, and the terrible bottom. Such is the perennial human story of the fall from purity into dissipation and death.

The little boy in the storybook felt that if he did not grasp Scuffy before the boat entered the ocean, then there would be a lonely, tragic, and desolate ending. Every spiritual child feels a primal fear that whatever is most precious and loved is in danger of disappearing forever into a vast and merciless chaos. To live a joyful life we must grasp the story, not the toy.

Water pouring into the sea can only return in one possible way, and that is to transpire. It must be lifted by the sun and join a great cloud; it must float and move with the wind, until it condenses and rains down again. But who would believe such a story?

To live a joyful life one must move as God's grace from heaven to earth. One must flow downward like the water seeking the lowest place. When coming to land's end, one must not fear to be grasped. One must be lifted by the Son and carried into the cloud of witnesses and fellowship of saints. One must move with the Holy Spirit and be born into a new creation. But who would believe such a story?

Sock It To Me

"Socks! Wool socks," I emphasized. I felt like a traitor to the essence of childhood. As a boy, I could not believe in the sincerity of any adult who wanted socks for Christmas. Now I appreciate socks, especially the warm, woolly, stretchy kinds that won't crease your skin.

"Peace!" This was always the answer to my annual question, "Daddy, what do you want for Christmas?" His was an answer that would leave me standing there with my mouth open. I was ready to say, "What color?" or "What size?" and all I could think was, "What's he talking about?"

Only now do I appreciate his answer, with a sigh that binds my heart to my heavenly Father through my earthly father. Now I yearn for peace. I see peace for my grandchildren's lives as the greatest mission on earth. I see peace as the first and most precious gift the risen Lord breathes upon humanity.

Angels! They entice me at Christmas. I mean real extraterrestrial, Unidentified Flying Angels, a.k.a. UFAs. I await a power greater than my own. I seek heavenly intervention to confront our worldwide addiction to political, economic, and social abuses. I yearn for a change in reality, for an immense difference to become manifest.

Grace! When? When we have eaten all we can eat? Drunk all we can drink? Bought all we can buy? Earned all we can earn? Thought all we can think? When will we be ready for grace? Will I embrace the long Advent night? Can I accept that it is time to be still and to let God be God? This would mean letting myself be merely human, an incomplete creature who is chronically under construction.

I thought I was a sovereign individual, but really I am an opened-ended process, an unfinished project. I thought that I would get control over my life, but find that I am continually subject to what happens around me. In truth, I am continually being informed and reformed by dynamic powers over which I have no authority. I thought I would become a complete adult, but I find myself like a baby, still in the womb and being knit together by numerous, unknowable agencies. For now I feel my resistance to peace, angels, and grace. If I allow God to inform me, then I must be vulnerable to change and lacking in self-determination.

My Christmas list is shrinking down toward socks. Could this be a depressing indication that I am resigning myself to a world that will never satisfy my values? Or could it mean that I am about done with seeking high-end substitutions for God?

I may no longer be attempting to stuff the place that my sould should occupy with lots of stuff that never satisfies. Perhaps I am getting ready to appreciate the grace of the Christ child. If I am preparing for death, I would try to get as much into my life as possible. If I am preparing for a birth, I must clear out as much as I can to make room for a new creation. For which are you preparing? What does your Christmas list say?

Suppose

Suppose someone gives you a small cup and says, "Please get me a drink of water from Niagara Falls." How could you get one small cup of water from the tons that thunder down?

Suppose you are a physician. You have gone through college, medical school, and residency. A patient comes to you in great misery; he has complex symptoms, only some of which relate to your area of expertise. In addition to the complicated medical problems, the patient has significant work stress, unhealthy personal habits, financial difficulties, and ambivalence about getting well. How do you help him to heal?

Suppose you have billions of dollars to give to victims of terrorism. You must divide these funds among those who lost loved ones, those who were injured, those who came to the rescue, and those who lost employment. Do you give more money to those without insurance? Do you give more to those who had a higher incomes, so they can continue in the same way? Do you give to people who might spend it all at once and not use it wisely? Do you go about making people fill out long forms so you can judge and control each one? How do you distribute billions of dollars?

Suppose you are shopping for a Christmas gift. You scour the mall, looking at thousands of items.

Would she like this? Would it fit? Is the color right? Is it affordable? Does she already have one of these? How can you be sure to pick out a gift she would really appreciate from among the numerous possibilities?

Suppose you love someone, and you want to give him that message of love. Suppose that person is suspicious, having been ignored, abused, criticized, and discouraged throughout childhood. How can you convincingly say "I love you" to someone who doubts that he is loveable?

Are not many of the things you are supposed to do impossible? Or are they more possible than you think. Perhaps because you can't be God, you have stopped offering whatever you can give.

Your presence may be the Christmas present that God would give to someone. Perhaps a plastic cup that you hold up to dry lips would pour out more love than Niagara Falls.

Tight Receivers

Faithful Church members frequently have difficulty learning to receive. Because the Church needs our time for ministry and our money for survival, we rarely emphasize "receiving."

With a lack of attention toward receiving, many of us become trained to receive the wrong things, at the wrong time, and in a wrong way. We receive life, but live in fear of death. We receive knowledge, but press ahead toward the time when we will be free of education. We receive wisdom, but can't wait for the sermon to end. Even when we receive an abundance of things, our attention strays toward what others have. How does a world so weak at receiving embrace the birth of Christ? Often it doesn't.

I often struggle with this. I thought I would sit down for a half hour to occupy myself completely with our Lord as my Christmas gift. Even as I was thinking this, I was heading for a cup of coffee. I was going to receive the coffee first, and then get back to the Christ baby. Surely no earthly baby would let me get away with this kind of delay. Neither a baby nor the God that created him takes second place to a brown brew.

I really enjoy brief opportunities to hold babies. Long and extended opportunities can sometimes be a significant challenge, a spiritual education. Babies receive all the affection, attention, and energy we can give them. A baby never says, "Don't bother. That's too much trouble." Babies never doubt that they are completely worthy of consuming all your effort, care, time, and love. They are not embarrassed to be total receivers.

"Except you receive the Kingdom of God like a little child," says Jesus, "you shall not enter therein." The Kingdom of God is too great to be squeezed in between a cup of coffee and writing a Christmas book. I am a miserly, parsimonious, and resistant receiver. Like many others, I allow God only short times and little spaces to give me the immense spiritual gifts that divine grace seeks to bestow. How can God fit the fullness of divine beauty, truth and love into the meager space-time that I offer?

Christmas is the right time for us to practice the art of receiving a gift. This gift is so great that I could spend my whole life seeking to receive it and still miss more than I grasp. The Christmas gift of God takes forever to appreciate, but that is why we are given eternal life.

Faith is Fun

I attended a seminary where the refectory walls were lined with portraits of serious and stern scholars. One portrait was of a biblical professor in the 1800's whose lectures were long forgotten, but whose name was famous. He was Clement Clarke Moore, the man traditionally credited with writing the poem "A Visit from Saint Nicholas" as a special Christmas gift to his ill child.

Life for Santa is not all fairy-tale existence

Today this poem is more commonly known as

"Twas the Night Before Christmas." Its vision of a jolly toy giver who drives a reindeer sleigh and slides down chimneys rapidly became the accepted image of Santa Claus. For some, however, this new image became "the treason of the season." In reaction, attempts to "put Christ back in Christmas" began and such efforts continue to this day.

In a culture that spends many times more on celebrating Christ's birthday than on practicing Christ's religion, it can hardly be doubted that sore feelings about Santa Claus reside in the Church. About a quarter of all retail sales take place at Christmastime, as we buy and exchange birthday presents that presumably belong to the Lord. Sour grapes are pressed in many cheerfully decorated pulpits.

Before we make ourselves into 'anti-Santas' and miserable Scrooges, we should contemplate why we are driven to commercial excess. We are starved for things of brightness and times of fun. We need excuses to be happy and to spend time with one another. We want to share and enjoy life together, but we are usually doing what we call "more important things."

The problem is not that Santa Claus has stolen Christmas. The problem is that we are spiritually too ill to grow out of childish wants and embrace a childlike soul. Why do we not appreciate daily what is our brightest and best reality? Why don't we make merry with our friends and families all the time? Why is not every encounter with a child taken as a chance to say something silly and to fake a funny dance? Why do we normally keep our distance from those closest to us? Santa stories and poems usually teach tender affection and end with some communion of hugs and cookies.

Santa Claus need not be trivial. Often what he represents is a vast improvement over the numerous days we waste being serious and overworking to achieve prideful goals. God the Creator — who made quasars and quarks, who invented toddlers and watermelons, and who provides the original material for funny cartoons and pesky puppies — must have a sense of humor.

Children of God play naturally with God. Faith is fun. It is sin that bites. Let's put the fun back into Christmas. Learning to enjoy God's children now is the education that prepares us to enjoy one another in heaven forever.

Child Power

The world has ended many times. For St. Paul's Cathedral it has ended at least twice in the last thirty years. In the early 1980's urban blight led to a chronically leaking roof that destroyed our interior walls. In 1995 the bombing of the Alfred P. Murrah Federal Building blew us apart, closing the Cathedral and Parish House for three years.

Endings tell us much about the things that continue. They tell us about the tenacious faith, courage, and suffering that endurance demands. They also reveal that no technology, theology, or organization can remove the cross from the way, the truth, or the life.

During an interview on TV, a renowned artist told how offended he was at the birth of his daughter. He complained of the painful amount of energy and effort that he invested to create his works of art. Despite all of his efforts, his most glorious creation was his little girl, who had required no artistic talent or labor on his part whatsoever. The graciousness of God is so unfair!

For many God's graciousness is worse than unfair; it is morally offensive. How could God allow millions of children to die from the sinful actions and inactions of adults? The permissiveness of God is a terrible scandal. God does not even zap us when we have the nerve to fight with one another over our incompetent, but nevertheless competitive, moral superiorities.

Margaret works as a nurse on a maternity ward, so we have daily accounts of human behavior at times of birth. While there have been significant medical advances, there also have been substantial spiritual regressions. After a few minutes of ogling the newborn, the mother gets on with her cell phone calls as the father returns to the important sports event on TV.

When the parents share their feelings with staff, they often flow along predictable channels: physical discomfort, lack of sleep, financial stress, and interpersonal conflicts. The presence of a baby becomes an additional problem in an already stressful world. Many appear glad to leave the hospital, but seem sorry to go home.

This behavior pattern also dominates how our culture keeps Christmas. We spend a small time in true appreciation, but we are soon distracted by fussing, shopping, decorating, and discussing our nearest-and-dearest family of problems. We are glad to leave home for parties, but feel sorry for too much food and small talk.

The first Christmas was glorious in spite of taxes, barnyard odors, and Herod's malice. Christmas in Oklahoma was beautiful in 1983 even though the walls were a mess and the finances miserable. Christmas 1995 was profound in Dean Willey Hall, despite broken hearts filling a broken room. Each ending has been another beginning.

All issues and adults become old. While the world is always dismembering what we have been, God faithfully remembers who each precious child is born to be. The divine Christmas gift is reissued not to acceptable adults, but to all who accept the power to become God's children.

Primal Lover

All of us want to be loved, not for what we accomplish, but for who we are. Trying to achieve a great Christmas, like trying to make someone love you for what you do, leads to frustration. Allowing Christmas to become alive is like allowing a loved one to be free.

Jesus taught in his time that man was not made for the Sabbath, but the Sabbath was made for man. We should approach Christmas in this same way. God made Christmas for all humanity. Everyone who receives Christmas as a gracious gift receives it as a child of God rather than as an achiever of goals.

The baby is the icon of primal love, and creation is the vehicle for that love. Having faith means trusting that I can be loved as a baby is loved: because I am here, I belong, and I am connected in some deep and miraculous way to you and God. This is faith in the source and power of love. Like a baby, trust your Creator and allow the time and the space to be loved.

Earned affection, which comes from what I do, is important, but less so than primal love. Earned love is the love expressed through labor and responsibility. It may be willed, made, and performed. It is rational love; my lovely actions leading to your lovely responses. This is fair love, justice love, and the relative love of loving your neighbor as your self. It is always a secondary expression of the original and primal love of God.

Unlike earned love, primal love cannot be achieved through secondary means. The world loves you, or fails to love you, for just and unjust causes. God loves you because God loves you.

Many rational, intelligent people become holiday-weary from trying to manipulate their thoughts, feelings, and experiences to create a meaningful Christmas. The paradox is that Christmas is only special and unique because it is unachievable by mere human effort.

When hassled by a world that comes at you forcefully, do not defend yourself by filling your life with busyness and things. Allow your Creator to approach you and to minister to you, as a parent would comfort a small child. Allowing empty space and time to be invisibly blessed requires courage, humility, and patience. Whenever we act first, we make God second. Let God be the Primal Lover, the First Person, and the One who moves.

> *I still my soul and make it quiet,*
> *like a child upon its mother's breast*
> *my soul is quieted within me.* (Psalm 131:3)

We are called to love God with all our heart, mind, soul, and strength, because God is all and whole. We may express God's love for our neighbor and our selves in the parts and pieces of daily reality that come under our small domain. God does not reject our hard work and achievements, but honors our efforts to give and to create, just as a parent honors the Christmas gifts of a child. Such honor comes not from the value of our gifts, but from the value of the child who offers a gift.

Our souls yearn for the first, pure, and primal Lover. Primal love is the fountain of youth, from which one is continually made God's child.

Christmas Music

I was in the music department of a bookstore looking at the collection of Bach recordings. I pondered the different sounds hidden beneath the colorful CD jackets. I thought about how many music discs I already owned, but how few I regularly played.

There are certain works to which I often return, but a large amount of my music abides in the dusty silence of the shelf. Is anything wrong with this music? No, of course not. Many of my albums are excellent productions, featuring great composers and talented artists.

I could have comforted myself with the thought that I am a very busy person who has but a few minutes to spare for the luxury of listening. But then why was I here, cruising the CD aisles? I had hundreds of discs at home that went daily without love and attention! Why didn't I appreciate them? Why was I considering spending money on more music?

I began to think about how much work goes into appreciating good music. It is much easier to select, to buy, and to abandon a piece of music than to get to know it as a child knows a favorite story. Many of us, however, lack the discipline to commit the active and personal attention that is essential to appreciating new and unfamiliar sounds.

On a first listening, classical music is often harder to appreciate than pop music. Likewise, historical forms of worship are more difficult to embrace than newer, multi-media forms of worship. It requires significant commitment and active, personal attention to see the wisdom of the centuries slowly unfold week after week, year after year. The seasonal liturgies and the treasure of church music require decades of moving through ear, mind, and heart to be fully appreciated.

Music that is centuries old has filtered through the hearts and minds, the ears and instruments, of numerous musicians. They have selected from a vast quantity of musical possibilities the most exquisite pieces to play again and again. If you learn to delight in such ancient spiritual treasures, you will become like the wise person in the Gospel, the one who takes from the treasure in his closet both what is new and what is old. You will continue historic traditions that share this source of great joy across time.

Those who uncover this found-fortune will feel truly blessed. They will also conserve this cultural wealth for those who follow them. They are evangelists of sublime sounds in a world that tends to amplify noise with amazing technical skill. Like the beautiful feet of messengers who carry good news across the mountains, beautiful music of consolation and peace carries blessings over the rocks of sin, grief, and worldly dissonance.

Through the tiny mechanism of the human eardrum, we can access much more of God's glory than our mind can — or should — reduce to words. The one who listens to Bach discovers not only magnificent music, but also hears the resounding power of God's love and grace.

Listening to music opens a passage that leads through the humdrum of the world and through the ear drums of our bodies to reach the depths of our hearts. Christmas music is about God using earthly materials for heavenly purposes. Christmas is about God accessing the human soul through the most delicate, sensitive, and beautiful of all creations, a newborn baby.

Anne Kueteman's drawing of Canon Raab rehearsing a St. Paul's Cathedral Choir

Potato Party

A news program showed a French soldier placing a bag of potatoes in the lap of a young peasant refugee. Her eyes brightened as a smile of joy and relief spread across her face.

At her age, had I received a sack of potatoes for Christmas, I would have considered it child abuse. At my present age, I realize that I still take for granted that God will answer my daily prayer for daily bread. The Lord has given me so much that it is difficult to accept merely potatoes or bread as blessings.

Ashley Brilliant remarked, "It is the luxuries I need, the necessities I can live without." This is the terrible humor of our human condition. We have become addicted to our own personal luxuries, which have become necessities.

Although we do it day after day, we never tire of eating our own daily meals; yet sometimes we tire of the poor, who have the audacity to become hungry again and again. Christmas reminds us that Jesus spent his early years moving as a refugee through Egypt. The Gospel promises that the Christ child is still to be found among those who hunger and thirst.

Gospel servants serve the bodily needs of the children of God. Parish food pantries must be centers of communion. Since the Lord has promised to be among the least of those who are fed, then no doubt angels, archangels, and the host of heaven can be found here.

Throughout the ages, scholars and philosophers have discussed that we are who we think we are. "I think, therefore I am" was Descartes' statement when he concluded that thought exists. Church authorities have spent centuries bickering over who should be in communion with one another. Many believe that the belief in our heads — that is, what we think — is the primary criteria for qualifying or disqualifying a person to eat a particular denominational brand of sacramental bread.

There is an ancient saying, "All food is the love of God made edible." A church pantry might offer to a hungry person the love of God made tangible in a warm greeting, a few groceries, and a bus pass. Many scoffers see both this small aid and sacramental feeding as mere tokenism. Yet it is through small and common things that the Most High daily touches humanity. Since qualifying for food at a pantry primarily depends upon the Gospel criteria of being hungry, food pantries may have something to teach theologians.

May God bless all the faithful volunteers and laborers

who multiply their Creator's generosity by using their own hands to fill the empty with good things. Those who serve in this way bring to us a foretaste of heaven, where guests pour in from east and west, north and south, and where they sit at banquet in the presence of the Lord.

In his parables Jesus continually speaks about God as a party giver. The Gospel bids us to invite people into our homes and to share life together. To paraphrase an old proverb regarding what to serve, "Better potatoes eaten with joy, than prime ribs cooked with aggravation."

Clarity

"Let me make this clear," promised Richard Nixon frequently. What he always meant was, "Let me make this definite." This is the way it is! Attempting to make his re-election definite cost him his presidency.

"Let me make this unclear" is something I never promise, but frequently achieve. Bear with me, and many presumptions about clarity will become unclear.

"Let me make this perfectly clear!"

A person recently told me a story about a flight where the pilot announced, "I uh, uh … believe … we are going to … St. Louis." This did not inspire confidence. One person heard from the pilot that he was distracted; another that he was comical; still another that he was a distracted comedian.

What was evident was the numerous possibilities of interpreting the pilot's words. "The sky was the limit" to transparent speculations.

Clarity-as-transparency provides numerous levels of truth. The fullest possibilities are found in the language of mythic, poetic, and narrative stories. The language with the smallest tolerance for ambiguity is also the one most fussy about definition: mathematics. Rare are the minds that can tolerate the precision of mathematical thought.

Still waters are transparent. You can see through quiet water into rich depths. Turbulent waters are opaque. You can see colors and motion on the surface, but you cannot look through such water to deeper things. For centuries mystics have observed the same truth in humans. Clarity of expression requires a quietness and stillness of mind.

As you approach the great feast of Christmas, will you try to get everything right and over with as painlessly as possible? When some Christmas story moves you, will you rebuke yourself for being silly and sentimental? If you don't feel such things, will you feel disappointed, cold, and isolated? Will you explain away as foible and folly the great range of emotions provided by our Creator to all who are fully alive? The depth of sorrows and the heights of joy are one ride.

Pray for your heart to hear heaven through the familiar melody of a Christmas carol; to see heaven through the excited eyes of a child; to thank heaven through the bright lights of a warm home; and to know heaven is near in the tear for a missing, beloved soul.

A rationally efficient God would have dropped a complete thousand-page manual of precise theological details from the sky and stayed safely uninvolved with this gross world. Why bother with a baby, a story, angelic music, shepherds, Magi, and a complicated cast of humans and animals? Those who see through these artificial devices know that all God-fabricated reality is clearly an excuse to stage pageants of divine love.

Have A Great Body

As Margaret was leaving the supermarket, she chatted with the man helping her with the bags. She asked, "What are your plans for Christmas?" He replied, "I can't wait 'til it's over. When I get off work I am going to get a six pack and watch TV until I fall asleep."

Some people dream of a white Christmas, but many

more expect to endure an empty, isolated holiday aided by some instruments of stupefaction. This is nothing new.

Samuel Johnson tells how Alexander the Great, at the height of his power, needed to drink himself to sleep with wine. His body could not be at peace with the glory of his achievements. He had arrived at stardom; he was too brilliant to let himself be at rest in the darkness. There was always too much to do: another campaign to plan, another strategy to conceive, another threat to avoid.

Humanity has invented an increasing variety of distractions to dim the divine light that shines within every person who enters this world. Besides drugs and alcohol, the world offers us numerous products to blur our awareness and suppress the bright child-soul that burns within us. Individuals and communities alike struggle to embrace the abundant aliveness inherent in the primal gift of life.

We struggle as a parish community to be a place of presence — to be a responsive corporate body that ministers to the needs of those we encounter. To be fully alive in community is to be in constant motion, resounding from the depths of human pain and sorrow to the heights and delights of earthly and heavenly joys. As a fish outside of water is a pathetic critter, so is a human being outside a thriving community.

Sometimes churches resist life and motion. Parishes act as if the people who comprise and surround the parish do not exist. The church as a corporate body must learn like human bodies learn. Humans learn and grow by doing things, not by thinking about things. The corporate body learns to pray, to worship, to visit the sick, to feed the hungry, and to adore God by doing these activities. The corporate body, like a child, is capable of embodying both childlike enthusiasm and reverent discipline.

The Body of Christ today, as on the first Christmas two thousand years ago, abides in flesh. We gather as a body of bodies to be alive, share, suffer, care, love, help, learn, labor, and pray.

What are your plans for Christmas? I hope you will not bind your body to a TV and a six-pack. Be free to be somebody in the presence of other bodies. To share a community body with a Christ-child soul means to have a great body.

One Light

A young college student said to me, "If God is everywhere, why am I so lonely?" A theologian might rephrase the question, "If God is everywhere all the time, what is the big deal about Christmas Day?" Is not one day as good as another? Is not every day Christmas?

The student's question was not for a theologian, but for a pastor. His was a personal plea. Why am I so lonely? If God is everywhere, why am I missing out?

Many people feel this question most deeply at Christmastime. They see Christmas everywhere around them, but it is not "taking place" in their lives. Many people feel no sacred time; they find no Holy Day Inn for their soul. Some grow frustrated in their efforts "to make the Christmas" they cannot locate.

C.S. Lewis described Narnia as a place where it is always winter, but never Christmas. This is a common experience for many people. They decorate elaborately and go to parties, but Christmas never comes. A birthday party without a birth lacks that special someone.

The young student was disappointed that God was not accessible to him twenty-four/seven as many theologians advertise. A hard lesson for every child to learn is that she or he must wait until December 25.

The student felt lonely because he found emptiness where the divine presence is supposed to be. "Lonely" is a word rooted in the word "one." The word "alone" comes from the two words "all one." The one at the center of lonely and alone is the One the young man was missing.

Taking our loneliness to this One is called prayer. Sharing our all-oneness with humanity in the presence of God is called Holy Communion. The spiritual journeys from our multitude of self-centers toward the One is an immense, and for most of us, long-term adventure.

Mary and Joseph, shepherds and Magi all had to go out of their way to get to Christmas. Getting out of my self and getting serious about prayer is one part of a multifaceted spiritual journey. Most of us must travel all the way from the absence of soul to the presence of God. This means starting not from where we should be, but from where we miss the point. That is why most religions talk about beginning with repentance and change.

Most of my thinking is a process of hiding in the loneliness of my brain to escape from the tangible reality that challenges my soul. A.A. groups call this "stinkin' thinkin'." How can I find Christmas—divinity in humanity—if I do not engage my human condition in flesh and blood?

The Christmas Gospel proclaims that the primal Word of God is "the light that lights all people" (John 1:4). God is the One present in everyone. When my light is God's Light, graciousness and truth become all One, and loneliness vanishes with the darkness.

Many nations and races, one light and one love.

Recovering Light from the Bottom of Darkness

For many of us, the bright lights and merriness of the Christmas season only make the dark areas of our lives more obvious. When this happens, we connect to the reality that the Christ child was born into times of tyranny and terror. It is important to realize how deep into such darkness the Christmas story journeys and how difficult and essential it is to follow its path.

The Christmas story tells of Mary and Joseph fleeing into the night to evade oppressors. The infant Jesus must remain hidden, like a newborn fawn in a predatory environment. The shepherds and the Magi must search through the night to find baby Jesus. This holy night is for discovering what cannot be seen in the daylight.

Classic medieval mystics, such as St. John of the Cross and St. Theresa of Avila, spoke about the Dark Night of the Soul. In the Dark Night, the God they imagined in the brightness of their rational thought is absent. In darkness, ideas about God appear vacant and lost, and human affection for God seems hollow and conditional. The God who we thought we knew in the daylight becomes the One unknown and ungraspable in the darkness. In this night, we find not the God we have been seeking, but the One we have refused to see.

Tourists usually travel by day to see the sights. Spiritual tourists visit inspiring places; they stop and ponder by trees or water; and at day's end they turn on a lamp to read their spiritual books. By contrast, the shepherds and Magi traveled at night. They looked for what was invisible in plain daylight. They sought not what was known, but what was unknown.

Many spiritual tourists have briefly glimpsed a light and then spent their days compelling others to see it. They describe their beliefs and ideas with a definitive certainty that many others find difficult to embrace. Like tourists who explain every travel photo in exasperating detail, those who share their spiritual beliefs and ideas quickly grow wearisome. The tourist seeks what is on his itinerary, while the pilgrim looks more deeply for what no eye may see, no ear may hear, and no itinerary may list.

On a black, moonless night you can best see the starry immensity of the universe. When you see the vastness of billions of stars, how can you ever know where you are? The traditional manner of finding the star above you in the sky is to look into a deep well. If you look down into the quiet, dark well water, you will see reflected the light that is directly overhead. So it is that by looking down silently and fearlessly into your self that you can discover the light from on High that abides in both body and mind.

When I was about thirteen I was swimming from a

small boat on Long Island Sound. Trying out a new mask, snorkel, and flippers, I decided to find out how far underwater I could go. I took a full breath and started down with all my energy. When I could go no farther, I had a sudden pang that bordered on panic. I could not see where I was, and I was surrounded only by the immensity of shiny, dark, gray water. I could not tell what direction was up. As desperate as I was to bolt toward the surface for a breath, I had to wait for the buoyancy of my body to bring me to the surface.

A touch of that traumatic moment returns when I am over-my-head in some threatening, unknown situation. The challenge to be still abides as an act of faith. In silent prayer I find my soul rises in the presence of God as naturally as my body rose that day in the ocean.

It is from the consequences of our machinations or those of others that we often need the most help. The alcoholic taking her first steps toward sobriety moves through the dark unknown, relying upon a Higher Power for both her will and her way. By acknowledging her condition, looking into its depths, and pausing in the flood of lies she tells herself and others, the alcoholic allows her soul to arise toward a Higher Power. It is by facing the truth of the pig pits that the prodigal son comes to himself and arises to go to his father. It is from the depths of darkness that our soul calls upon God and permits truth to emerge. Help is not delivered through a manual of ideas on how to save ourselves. Salvation is a divine presence, one that uplifts us more naturally and gracefully than the force of earth's gravity draws us down.

The recovery of our souls, like the healing of our bodies, takes place below our conscious surface. Surface knowledge is neither the soul's goal nor the heart's treasure. Instead, we seek the awareness of divine love that is given as the ultimate Christmas present. The Bethlehem manger is about the presence of the Highest in the impoverished depths of our human condition. In the traditional words of Mary, the Lord's greatest gift allows the lowest souls to magnify the highest God.

Terror & The Innocents

Many years ago I held a Bible study group in a prison. One of the inmates brought up the Murder of the Holy Innocents, when King Herod ordered all male children in Bethlehem executed. The convict said that God was responsible for these murders because he had sent baby Jesus. He argued those children would have lived if God had not created these circumstances. Such a thorough rationality can justify almost any crime.

St. Paul's Cathedral closed by the
Murrah Building Bombing of April 19, 1995.

The murders of Amish schoolgirls in 2006 brought back memories of the night following the bombing of the Alfred P. Murrah Federal Building in Oklahoma City. From the morning the bomb detonated until some time after midnight, I was in frantic motion. Throughout the day new realizations of what had been shattered and destroyed challenged my body, mind, and spirit.

When I finally got into bed, I felt physically exhausted, but could not relax. I fell asleep briefly and then awoke with all sorts of worries. What happened to the woman with the blood-covered blouse after she ran back toward the Murrah building with oxygen canisters? Was our parish hall, with all the glass gone and only a half ceiling intact, functioning well enough to feed two-hundred rescue workers? Did we have enough food? Should I have stayed there? How would we ever afford to repair the stained glass and the damaged organ pipes?

Lying there half-awake, I saw the day's events transform. From a myriad of small, concrete details, there emerged primal and mythical dimensions. I kept seeing the rescue workers digging through the dark rubble. Like Tolkien's hobbits, they labored deep into the lair of the fire-breathing dragon. My mind squeezed into painful constrictions with them. Pangs moved through me as I felt them lift a mangled child and carry him like a sacred treasure.

We should have known this would happen. We, the peasant villagers, should have been alert. We should have been suspicious. How could we be so absorbed with the practical details of our lives that we missed the beast's entrance into our town? How could we be so out of touch and so unaware of impending evil? How could we leave the door to our hearts this unguarded? How could we allow a neo-Herod access to our Holy Innocents?

My descent into the rubble of the Murrah Building had driven me into hell and challenged my soul to come forth. Would I suppress such a devastating reality or wrestle with it until morning? If I could hold on until dawn, this struggle with terror might become a significant part of my soul's journey toward the light.

Like Jacob, I still wrestle in the darkness with whatever is confounding my soul. Nights are longer than when I was young. I spend more time awake, and I feel more grateful for the morning. The ultimate morning has yet to dawn; a full awakening has yet to be. Meanwhile, I share a profound reality with ancient peoples and contemporary strangers—everyone who has looked into the depths of terror and tragedy. Knowledge of good and evil has always meant facing the murder of innocence. No soul will journey long through this space-time without seeing the terrifying immensity of the world's night.

The wise will humbly seek every accessible point of light, whether from heaven or earth. Although we live in a secular culture, when some awful crime offends a community, our hearts move to light small candles and walk together through the dark times. The candle points flow like a river of stars shining in the blackness of the universe. Each tiny light carries a soul's message; each flame burns tenuously and tenderly, like the Christ infant's light flickering on the margins of a terrorized humanity.

In a world of contending forces, amid actions and reactions, large-scale causes and effects, and long-standing alienations and retaliations, there abides this little, delicate, immature possibility of divine love in the form of warm, fragile flesh. True-to-death stories are the purest form of truth. The Christmas story shows us that the way toward a divine comedy remains open, even in the darkest circumstances. God has given us an opportunity not only to co-author the story of our souls, but also to draw heavenly conclusions, even from a hell of a journey.

This is the Christmas altar of St. Paul's Cathedral celebrating our first Christmas upon return from exile.

Noisy Night

Imagine singing these words to the tune of "Silent Night":

Noisy day, restless day,
All is tense, all uptight
'Round the house is mess and grime
Nothing works, there is no time
Force an unearthly pace,
Force an unearthly pace.

Imagine sitting down with a three-year-old to explain the family finances. "Mommy has to send checks to the mortgage company and the electric company so that we can have a nice, warm house to live in." Or try justifying to a seven-month-old, "Daddy didn't mean to scream in your ear, but he had his hands full, and your brother was running toward the street, and he was already late and overwhelmed by too many things to do." The baby would only give you that wonderful look that merely says, "You're my Daddy! I forget everything else."

Parents cannot explain the hardness of the world to their children anymore than the children can put their hurt feelings into words. A robotically rational child might say, "Parental figure, in our current socio-economic level, the proportion of our dysfunction to our discomfort is well within the probabilities of the prevailing statistical data. Besides which, all noise is the same as music. Chill!"

The stress upon Mary, Joseph, and baby Jesus was considerably more than most families encounter on Christmas. They traveled late into Mary's pregnancy, not to visit family, but to pay taxes. They could find no suitable shelter. Then they were forced to leave abruptly because of the terror of Herod.

'The Flight Into Egypt by Don Lorenzo Monaco'

God does not provide a detailed or rational explanation for why the life of the Holy Family was so hard. Even today, the dysfunction and discomfort of a hostile world continues to threaten every small gathering of human warmth, affection, and intimacy. It is in the midst of the cold, dark night that the warmth of divine love takes place.

The world is a frightening and dangerous place for God's children of all ages, yet children find numerous resting places. Home this moment may be a hovel, a mansion, or a donkey's back. It is the human context of the family, not the quality of the space, that makes the most difference to a child.

We are all spiritual migrants. Every place is a

temporary place. No matter how secure and beautiful we make any house, we must eventually move on from it.

This is also true of Christmas. We cannot construct a great Christmas holiday out of stuff. Christmas, like the refugee Holy family, moves across space-time. The old times and previous places are mostly past. Each Christmas must be made from the opportunities that are present, in whatever time and place the travelers find themselves. For the adult soul, as for each small child, it will be the immediate human context from which this Christmas will emerge.

When Jerusalem fell and the Hebrews were exiled to Babylon, they lost their Temple and their calendar of worship. They could carry with them only the words in their books and their commitment to the holiness of the Sabbath day. So it is for us. When every Christmas symbol has been cashed or trashed or received the "kitsch of death," we still find a way through.

The aliveness of our souls and our awareness of holiness tenaciously endures, even when confronted by a hostile culture of noisy mockeries and forced merriness. Christmas carols abide as durable, portable sacred treasures. The darkness has no power to overwhelm the Silent Night.

Silent Night, Holy Night,
All is calm, all is bright,
Round yon virgin mother and child,
Holy infant, so tender and mild,
Sleep in heavenly peace.
Sleep in heavenly peace.

At Home

I remember Margaret, the children, and I celebrating our third Christmas in Oklahoma. It was such a blessing to be at home. Being "at home" is a quality of the spirit, not a consequence of geography. If you are at home, it means you are where you belong.

At Christmas many of us send cards and letters to people we will be unable to see. This gives us a sense of communion that bridges our spatial separations. As time marches on and Christmases come and go, the holiday begins to embody not only our expectations, but also our memories—the changes and the losses. We remember special times, particular old tattered ornaments, and certain unique gifts from days that can never be again. Some family traditions end. Sometimes we glimpse the strange endurance of childishness—a child whose eyes once opened wide in awe of bright lights—has now matured and frets over wasted electricity.

As bad world events become "our history," and family members become tender memories, the joy of Christmas is challenged at a core level. Our bright childlike imaginations, which once withstood the lengthening winter nights, now flicker like a candle flame struggling against a cold draft. Mere mementos, symbols, and decorations cannot uphold the human spirit. Multiplying the tinsel and finding the perfect ornament will not heal the heart's grieving.

Being "at home" for Christmas means being at the place where this world gives way to a whole other reality. Christmas is not sustained by things, by objects of glass and plastic but by the meanings those objects bear. The ephemeral importance of these objects brings us home to the first Christmas family–who had no home!

Being at home for Christmas does not mean sharing the same house; it means sharing homelessness with the saints who walked through long nights toward the Light. It means keeping our eyes open above, toward the heavenly brightness that guides us. It means keeping our hearts open to the numerous fellow souls we will encounter on our journey, and being ready to share Christmas warmth and cheer.

Being at home for Christmas means being alive to those who have died, with a fresh tear; it means being close to those who are far away, with a thought and a call. For the young, it means being in touch with an ancient heritage. For the old, it means being in touch with the new and the young.

Being at home for Christmas means turning toward the light that shines in every person who has come into the world. It means accepting the self who God created out of disposable flesh and blood. It means accepting corporeality and mortality, accepting God incarnate in the passing, temporary, and peculiar reality of humanity.

Being at home for Christmas means being in the fellowship of the body of humanity on earth, one of the crowd that squeezes into a pew. Being at home means being among the flowers, carols, and prayers, making joyful noises with the body we are given. It means worshipping a God who is not too proud to share divine life, love, and presence. Everyone who comes home for Christmas will find that Christmas is "the place" that is filled with the Children of God.

Our family home for twenty years. In memory and sentiment a great mansion of happy feelings. In wood and plumbing, a dilapidation from which we needed to be rescued and set free.

"Fa-la-la-ing"

Fa-la-la-la-la-la-la-la-la

What is it that allows serious humans to sing these words? To allow yourself to make such "fa-la-la-ing" sounds in public, with a whole heart, you need to be surrounded by a cheerful mass of voices willing "to folly" along. Choirs spend almost twenty notes just on the *glo* in "Gloria." To sing beautifully involves listening more than thinking. Thinking tends to embarrass and inhibit joyful impulses.

The child in us is enticed by long Latin phrases, nonsense noises, and strings of silly syllables. Christmas encourages us to babble freely, like a fresh brook bubbling through the rocks of old reality. Through our songs, are we not playing with the primal sounds that are rooted in our deepest origins?

Can you remember a place where there were no "mean" words? Can you think about a time before words existed, where sounds only played and teased with meanings? Imagine being alive before the knowledge of good and evil, before the discrimination of one word from another. To regress toward hearing pure sound is like returning to the beginning of creation where the divine Word sings reality into being.

And you will have joy and gladness, and many will rejoice at his birth. (Luke 1:14)

In Thailand, even in towns without any Christian community, people decorate and celebrate on December 25. Some people may just be responding to the media advertisements and hype that saturate our senses during this time of year. Some are celebrating a generic holiday in honor of a genuinely shared experience of newborn humans. The birth of Christ provides a good excuse to waste time and resources appreciating the improbable truth of human 'beingness'.

Humans are naturally drawn toward infants, regardless of their heritage. When the Egyptian princess saved the Hebrew baby Moses she was responding to something that transcended the brand names of race, class, creed, and rational self-interests. Many people experience an intimate communion with their divine origin when they express tenderness toward a baby. Babies inspire adoration, affection, joy, and enthusiasm in humane beings. The appeal is so basic that organizations and campaigns frequently use images of children to seek charitable responses.

How much time did you spend on *"Fa-la-la-la-la-la-la-la-la"* when you first saw it written above? Did you sing it out and remember the Christmas carol from which it comes? Or did your mind mechanically recognize *"Fa-la-la-la-la-la-la-la-la"* and then move on seeking more substantial thoughts? Why pause for such nonsense?

Poetry and music are divine gifts that extend the Christmas message through space-time. It takes only a small cue from an old song or poem to evoke the same great and joyful response as the day it was written. "Fa-la-la-la-la-la-la-la" gives Christmas duration across time and expression not bound to language. But only people who trust in abundant time, as in eternal life, are likely to feel the freedom of lavishing time on "Fa-la-la-ing."

Children learn to trust their parents long before they fully grasp the ideas and beliefs their parents are trying to pass along. Later in life, those children might consciously recognize that their parents had a particular childrearing philosophy or religious beliefs about family. They may come to adopt these values and ideas because their faith-trust was validated by parental love. A home where faith is proved true, is a home where joy abounds.

For everyone, but especially for those without a baby at home, Christmas is an opportunity to be in touch with the gift of soul within the mortal flesh of humanity. In celebrating the birth of Christ, you may hear the newborn who is within you babble and sing, and you may feel your insides dance for joy. You might even have some awareness of God's parental enjoyment of your joy.

Joy to the World

*Joy to the World,
the Lord is come!
Let earth receive her king!*

"Who wrote this hymn?"
   "… Watts's his name."

"What's-his-name wrote the hymn?!"
   "… Yes, Isaac Watts's his name!"

In the 1930's and 1940's the comedy team of Bud Abbott and Lou Costello delighted audiences by playing around with words in this way. Their career as a team ended prematurely — each performer confronted personal problems and illnesses, and Costello never fully recovered from the accidental drowning of an infant son. Despite their tragedies and flaws, the pair gave the world a gift of fun and laughter that is still enjoyed — even revered — to this day.

Joy in this world is often associated with delightful coincidences, happy inconsistencies, and funny confusions. Joy is not mechanical. It does not emerge from a cause-and-effect process. Instead, joy breaks out from the constraints of rational consistency; joy breaks the chains that bind miserable inputs to miserable outputs.

The verses of "Joy to the World" were written in 1719 by Isaac Watts, who had every reason to be enslaved by the chains of misery. He was raised in a strict Protestant tradition whose adherents were officially labeled in England as "Nonconformists," or "Dissenters." In that time and place, Christians who dissented from the Church of England were viewed with suspicion and disdain. Isaac's child-soul rebelled against this conflicted environment. Instead of being depressed, Isaac was irrationally, consistently, and gracefully happy. This contentious world was like a foreign land into which he could never assimilate.

As a young boy, Isaac had a great interest in writing verses. Once, during family prayers, he began to laugh. His father angrily asked him why. Isaac replied that he had heard a sound and opened his eyes to see a mouse climbing a rope in a corner. Isaac had immediately thought of the following:

> *A little mouse, for want of stairs,*
> *Ran up a rope to say its prayers.*

His father took this for irreverence and began to whip him. As he was being struck, Isaac pleaded,

> *Father, father, mercy take,*
> *And I will no more verses make.*

Obviously, little Isaac had lied. We know of Isaac Watts today because he versed and "re-versed" his whole life. By playing with words, even as an adult, Isaac accepted the power to become God's child.

Many adults seem to believe that words are primarily for making ideas that are better than their neighbor's ideas. People separate such ideas into true or false, right or wrong. Then they fight with one another, sometimes for centuries, over which is which.

The words of "Joy to the World" say it again and again: "Let heaven and nature sing!" These words tell us to let body and soul come together and celebrate. Jesus complained about those who resisted both the comedy and tragedy of being alive:

> *They are like children sitting in the marketplace and calling to one another, "We played the flute for you, and you did not dance; we wailed, and you did not weep."* (Luke 7:32)

For a brief time, Isaac Watts served as the pastor of a small congregation. However, the emotional rigors overwhelmed him, and he left the ministry ill and discouraged. It took the intervention of a wealthy benefactor to keep Watts from becoming a homeless vagrant. Watts went on to become one of the all-time great houseguests of history — he stayed with his host for thirty-six years!

Although hardly more than a beggar himself, Watts gave a third of his small allowance to the poor. His sensitivity to children and to the destitute, the most vulnerable and needful among us, is expressed in many of his hymns.

Watts's tenderness toward children was versed beautifully in *Divine Songs for Children*, published in 1715:

*Jesus shall reign wher e'er the sun
Doth its successive journeys run.
And infant voices shall proclaim
Their early blessings on His name.*

Watts lived during a time when theologies of "total depravity" were widespread. Many religious leaders taught that the world was entirely wicked, that creation had been completely corrupted. They said that no likeness existed between humanity and God the Creator, because it had been obliterated by sin. These preachers held that only their own belief system could provide truth that was not adulterated.

Today, we might consider that we, too, live in dark times. Many adults feel that they have a full comprehension of truth. But even among all the competing and varied ideologies — academic and popular, secular and religious — none has achieved, nor can ever achieve true unity, freedom, and peace for humanity on earth.

To see our world as full of immense possibilities rather than confining threats, we must become like a child. Doing this means giving up our adult illusions that we can ever "know enough" to impose our ideas upon others.

Adults engage babies with affectionate noises and faces, and they enjoy baby sounds and motions in response. The natural joy of a young child tells us that it is our primal nature to enjoy the presence of human beings. The Gospel tells us that there is more joy in heaven over one soul that participates in divine grace than over ninety-nine righteous souls who justify their misery. "Come ye faithful," and let God enjoy your soul enjoying Christmas.

> *Joy to the World!*
> *The Lord is come.*
> *Let earth receive her king;*
> *Let every heart*
> *Prepare him room*
> *And heav'n and nature sing,*
> *And heav'n and nature sing,*
> *And h-h-e-e-e-a-a-a-v'n and nature sing!*

ChristmasJoyBook.com

Sources

Front Cover - Figures used in collage from Plate 51 #490 Children A Pictorial Archive of Permission-Free Illustrations Carol Belanger Grafton Dover Press

Front Piece - 'Draggin' of Toomuchstuff' adapted from p. 31 Old Fashioned Christmas Illustrations by Carol Belanger Grafton Dover Press

Battle For Truth - Family photos

Will Christmas Ever Come? - Wiz, adapted from Public Domain Website

Barn Phew and Church Pew - Girl & Pig adapted from Plate 13 #131 Children A Pictorial Archive of Permission-Free Illustrations Carol Belanger Grafton Dover Press.

Womb Prayer - Family photo

Aidan & His Newborn Grandfather - Family photo

Baby As Spiritual Guide - Rembrandt's "Simeon" from Wikipedia Public Domain

Touching Baby Flesh - Sleeping Baby from iStock

Toddler Faith - Baby on Belly - iStock

Yes Virginia, Jesus Loves Santa Claus - Santa with Scissors adapted from p.24 Old Fashioned Christmas Illustrations by Carol Belanger Grafton Dover Press

Christmas Absent - Xmas Presents Bazaar – adapted from Plate 8 #072 Children A Pictorial Archive of Permission-Free Illustrations Carol Belanger Grafton Dover Press

A Dickens of a Christmas – Boy at window adapted from p. 24 Old Fashioned Christmas Illustrations by Carol Belanger Grafton Dover Press

Imagination - Family photo plus glove iStock

Scuffy - Tugboat on river from iStock

Sock It To Me - adapted from p. 10 Old Fashioned Christmas Illustrations by Carol Belanger Grafton Dover Press

Tight Receivers - Family photo

Faith Is Fun - Santa & Pantyhose adapted from p. 9 Old Fashioned Christmas Illustrations by Carol Belanger Grafton Dover Press

Christmas Music - Drawing by Anne Kueteman used by permission

Potato Party - from iStock

Clarity - Beast adapted from p. 23 #338 Full Color Medieval Ornament Dover Press

Have A Great Body - Troubled King from public domain web site; six-pack illustrated by Meredith Back

One Light - Photo from Cathedral Archive: Mission trip to Bolivia

Terror & the Innocents - Images from Cathedral Archives

Noisy Night - "Flight Into Egypt," Don Lorenzo Monaco, 004 - Wickipedia Public Domain

At Home - Family photo

Back Talk Santa and Back Talk Figure - David Coffey